FROM
UNDER
THE
Mulberry
TREE

FROM
UNDER
THE
Mulberry
TREE

D. CARVER BRAZWELL

ARCHWAY
PUBLISHING

Archway Publishing books may be ordered through booksellers or by contacting:

Archway Publishing
1663 Liberty Drive
Bloomington, IN 47403
www.archwaypublishing.com
1 (888) 242-5904

Because of the dynamic nature of the Internet, any web addresses or links contained in this book may have changed since publication and may no longer be valid. The views expressed in this work are solely those of the author and do not necessarily reflect the views of the publisher, and the publisher hereby disclaims any responsibility for them.

Any people depicted in stock imagery provided by Thinkstock are models, and such images are being used for illustrative purposes only. Certain stock imagery © Thinkstock.

ISBN: 978-1-4808-2092-0 (sc)
ISBN: 978-1-4808-2093-7 (e)

Library of Congress Control Number: 2015948345

Print information available on the last page.

Archway Publishing rev. date: 08/11/2015

To my Lord and Savior, The Christ.

Always eternal love for Damon and Lois Brazwell my parents.

To Glinda, Proverbs 31:10 Who can find a virtuous woman? for her price is far above rubies.

I could not find, so He gave you to me. God is very generous.

To my children Tomekka, Jeratio, and Bliss Chadwick, much love.

Special dedication to Tyler and young Mr. Myles, grandsons.

CONTENTS

A LONE STAR

A lone star from the eastern sky
Now shines over the Texas night
Made halo bright over the body of Christ
Down by the seashore.

A lone star hanging from the Texas sky
Casting shadows along the Rio Grande,
I follow the star across the Davis Mountains
On the trail of the buffalo.

A lone star is my guiding light
Across the dunes of the desert sea,
The body of Christ lay before me,
Resting against the sea.

A SILENT PLACE

A silent place you were dancing
In the midst of the maddening crowd
A place where worship abides in his splendor
A place created before mankind.
Dance with the one who loves you
Dance for the King of Glory
Dance for your Creator
Dance, dance, dance.
Your dance will tell your story
Of heartbreak, despair, and sorrow
Always dance a trail of remembrance
Of where he brought you from.
Dance for the one who sought you
Each step against the enemy who fought you
When you fail the King of Glory caught you
Through dance the King of Glory taught you.
Dance for those who lost hope
Your dance will break all the yokes
Dance and declare your victory
Dance for your past is just that, history.

A SMILE TO BRIGHTEN MY DAY

A smile to brighten my day,
Just one could do it so easily
Yet I know I will want more,
So don't hesitate,
Smile just one time
To brighten my day.

A smile that represents only you
Radiant, warm, so very loving,
It's a beautiful smile
And I adore it and you,
So come closer,
For to see and touch such beauty
Is a wondrous thought.

Afraid it will vanish
On a single touch,
Or break into many pieces upon the floor
Destroying my dreams if broken,
So always smile, you're beautiful.

A SONG FOR YOU

A song for you
Is a three-word tune
That I sing
Just from the thought of you,
A melody divine
I sing any old time
Darling, I love you.

I love you
Was composed for you
To sing just any old time,
I love you
Are the words
To my tune
Simple yet divine.

RAINDROP

A Texas-size raindrop
As big as a watermelon
Hangs from the Lone Star
Its drops are released from heaven.

A Texas-size raindrop
Can drown all sorrow
Big enough to float yesterday's defeats
Into victories of tomorrow.

A Texas-size raindrop
When it kisses the dirt
Mountains tremble willows weep
The earth begins to quake.

A Texas-size raindrop
Only falls from the Lone Star
I have one on my bookshelf
Held in a gallon jar.

ALL MUST PASS

All must pass
Through autumn's door
Where we are going
And have been before
All we do, say, and see,
Has passed before
Through autumn's door.

ALL THE SOUNDS

All the sounds
That silence makes
Whispered
But never said
It's the sea
Rushing the shore
A sudden wind
In forgotten lore
The moon when
It stains the night
A shadow overcast
That springs to life
It's a single bird
In lofty flight
The sunrise
After a stormy night
It's the gloom
In the northern sky
The first hello
The last good-bye
Whispered,
But seldom heard.

ACROSS TEXAS

Angel tears are falling across Texas
Tears of joy are covering the plains
From the Big Bend to the Red River Valley
Teardrops are falling out El Paso way.

Angel tears are falling across Texas
As we stroll the River Walk in Old San Antone
The Hill Country is alive with bluebonnets
As angel tears roll down its slopes.

Angel tears are falling across Texas
The pine trees of east Texas are dripping anew
The Trinity has swollen and crested
Flooded with angel tears crying *I love you*.

Angel tears are falling across Texas
I lift my face to receive from the Texas sky
Angel tears are falling across Texas
Another just fell from my eye.

GREEN EYE

As I look into
The liquid green eye
Of the sea
Memories of yesterday
Return to me
Castles built on the sand
Like our love
Were not built to last
The big red ball
Balanced on the sea
Like our love
In time
Departed from me.

AS IF IT NEVER WAS

As if it never was
The stream
Lost to the sea,
A journey
That changes with time,
As if it never was.

SUMMER DIES

As summer dies
So does the willow
It wept lonely tears
That reached to my pillow
It wept for the lazy days
That never will be forgotten
It wept for the summer breeze
That blew so softly
It wept for the moonlit nights
The fragrance of honeysuckle
It wept for the bird
It wept for the bee
It wept for the flower
It wept for me.

THE FIRELIGHT SLOWLY DIMS

As the firelight slowly dims
Reflections make puppets on the wall
Some are distant, but a few remain dear,
The others flee as I draw near.

I hear the crackle of the fire
It warms but the crackle sounds afar
I tune my ear to every word
The fire speaks to the shadows and says.

Dance with your wife and hold her near
Dance with the one who says, *I'll always love you, my dear*
Envelop her in the reflections that remain
Those reflections show her love will never change.

A reflection reaches out to me
And I withdraw as it reveals a tear to see
A tear that wets a trail to me
A tear destined for the sea.

As the reflections begin to fade
Embers flare and two reflections remain
Reflections dancing off firelight and sea,
Reflections of you and me.

THE GENTLE RAIN

As the gentle rain falls to earth
Each drop seeks to touch only you
Awakening the flowers, the trees, and me,
Each drop that touches only you.

Those single drops that fall on you
Travel through time and through me,
Like the flowers and trees
I yearn to sip, each drop that touches only you.

As the gentle rain falls to earth
Each drop forms a stream that flows to you
Wanting to touch you one last time
As they journey down to the sea.

CARRY ME BACK

Carry me back to Hobo Junction
Carry me back to my youth
We'll walk again down the blackberry patches
At night, watch the pine trees reach for the moon.

Carry me back to those bygone days
Carry me back real soon
We'll cast our lines from the shore
And where fishes really do swim in schools.

Carry me back to a summer day
I can smell the honeysuckle in full bloom
Carry me back to that faraway place
Carry me back real soon.

COME GO WITH ME

Come go with me
Where castles are made in the sand
A faraway place
That's close at hand
We will travel the universe
At a single glance
Nearness of the stars
Will light our path
A distant galaxy
Is our playground
In the sky
Come go with me
Never die.

FROM HEAVEN

Driven from heaven in a downpour,
With purpose sent from God to restore,
The earth received you with open arms,
Each drop embraced with thanks and love.

What a mighty river you have become,
Precious little raindrops that landed
At my front door,
As you passed with a mighty roar,
Another teardrop fell from heaven's door.

FALLEN LEAVES

Fallen leaves
From autumn's trees
Slowly fall from grace.

UNDER THE OLD OAK TREE

Five generations have walked under the old oak tree
Five generations including me
Five generations learned to stand as men under the old oak tree
Five generations including me
Five generations read the Bible and prayed under the old oak tree
Five generations including me
Five generations carved their names in the old oak tree
Five generations including me
Five generations were married under the old oak tree
Five generations including me
My son was born under the old oak tree
Six generations including he.

GOOD KEEPS IN A SECRET PLACE

God keeps in a secret place
Teardrops held in a sacred vase
There they are kept and lovingly stored
Until needed, then they are poured.
For the bride and groom, the newlyweds
For the grandfather lying on his sickbed
For all the lies that were said
Even for the newborn in his little crib bed.
I pour out my tear blessings upon you all
With love I guide each tear that falls
When they touch they cleanse and wash away
Neither lie nor death can take your place.
God keeps in a secret place
Teardrops held in a sacred vase
There they are kept and lovingly stored
Until needed, then they are poured.
For the daughter who has gone astray
For the son who stumbled and lost his way
For the father who would not stay
And for the mother who kneeled and prayed.
I pour out my tear blessings upon you all
Father, mother, daughter, and son
I saw how you cried last night through
One drop of this tear will cleanse all of you.
God keeps in a secret place
Teardrops held in a sacred vase
There they are kept and lovingly stored
Until needed, then they are poured.
For the mother who lost her only child
For the girl who has given up and cannot smile,
And for that brother trying to walk just one more mile
Hold your head up and begin to smile.

God keeps in a secret place
Teardrops held in a sacred vase
There they are kept and lovingly stored
Until needed, then they are poured.

GOD WATCH OVER ME

God, watch over me
My mouth, my ears
And the things I see.

No wagging tongue
Shall proceed before me,
God watches over me.

God, watch over me
My ears your voice do I seek
Your words are humble and make spirit meek
God watches over me.

God, watch over me
My eyes sometimes stray from thee
Your voice harkens and now I see
God watches over me.

GOLDEN LEAVES OF AUTUMN

Golden leaves of autumn
Prelude to a dreary past
Open the door for I come to rest
While life slows its symphony.

Golden leaves of autumn
You have taken my days of youth
For now I feel much older
With this shadow over me you have cast.

Gone are the summer breezes
Replaced with the chill of the north
Sunny days you have usurped
With rain and wintry storms.

I go and take my place beyond the dead
To wait until life is renewed
Swimming freely in languish thoughts
Of warmer days,
To start life anew

GREEN LEAVES

Green leaves
So fresh and new
Looking ever newer
From the morning dew
Shaking the wetness
Not long after dawn
Growing ever stronger
With the rising sun
Welcoming all travelers
For a noonday rest
Beautiful birds sing
While building their nest
Spring has opened its door
Mother nature will do the rest.

I GO WHERE THE DEWDROPS GATHER

I go where the dewdrops gather
Just beyond the silent sea
I go where echoing hearts reverberate
And tremble like windblown leaves.

I go where the whispers weep
And the winds gently carry beyond the clouds
I go where love has surrendered
And the wildflowers release a sigh.

I go where the nightingales sing
A mournful lullaby for the passing of June
I go where the rivers flow
And empty into the moon.

I go where the wind rages
And ravishes the old oak tree
I go where teardrops gather
They cry out, filling the silent sea.

A MIGHTY CLAP

I heard a mighty clap of thunder
As the angels came into view
Followed by a jarring blast
From the horn of Gabriel
I felt the passion of the Christ
As I stood before the gates of pearl
The angels in the presence of God
Marched together, two by two.

Two by two they appeared
On the streets paved of gold
Two by two they came forward
And bowed before the Throne
Two by two, as faces began to appear
Family, friends, and loved ones
Not a stranger among them
Nor did they shed a tear.

Two by two the angels opened the gates of pearl
Two by two the angels began to sing
As my family began to cheer
Two by two they led me before the throne of Grace
Another mighty clap of thunder
A voice rang out
Let the roll call begin.

My mother and father joined me
As Saint Peter called out my name
I bowed before the Throne of Grace
And Christ gave me my wings.

THE DAY SHE SAILED AWAY

I remember the day she sailed away
On a sea placid and calm
As she moved from the pier
The crowd let out a cheer
Someone shouted, "Good riddance
To the *Stormy O'Shea*!"
Stormy O'Shea, sleek and slim
The fastest ship on the Seven Seas
Stormy O'Shea has gone away
And taken with her my sweet Rosalie

A lone figure stood on a hill
Overlooking the bay
She did not move, just waved good-bye
As the ship sailed away
The crowd turned, as one they shouted,
"Look, there stands Stormy O'Shea
I looked with surprise at Stormy O'Shea
For there stood my sweet Rosalie
Like a dream she came forward
The crowd hushed, then parted
I cried "Rosalie," she heard not my plea
My beautiful swan then dove into the sea

Years later I walked the shore
Some say she will return one day
She'll change her name and won't look the same
But I'll know if it's my sweet Rosalie.

I REMEMBER WRITING

I remember writing
A love letter
In the sand
It washed away
With the tide
So I wrote it again
I remember the words
From that long-ago day
I kept writing
I love you
But it kept washing away
I kept writing the words
And didn't understand
Why *I love you* in the sand
Wouldn't last
But then I met JESUS
And behold
Now when I write
I love you
In the sand
It is written in stone.

THE ESSENCE OF YOU

I see the essence of you
Swirling through the wind
A leaf unfettered by time
Nor bound by branches of a tree.

I see the tumbleweed
Slowly rolling free
I think of you
Forever moving forward
With conviction and certainty.

You are like the cicada
Singing your song
In the midnight tree
Waiting for the wind
To carry you to your destiny.

Blow, mighty wind
As you take her from me
And when the journey is over
Mighty wind, safely return her to me.

I SET A CAGED BIRD FREE

I set a caged bird free,
Out of love
It departed from me,
Where it flew
I do not know
Only that it had to be free,
To sing a song of joy,
A song it could not sing,
Caged.

I TOLD THE OLD OAK A SECRET

I told the old oak a secret
Quietly so no other could hear
Thoughts from deep within
The old oak swayed and listened to me.

The old oak did not interrupt
It smiled and heard my plea
Then the old oak bent and whispered
Its leaves told of my family tree.

The old oak told of Great-Grandpa's struggles
Of keeping the family free
It told the horrors of slavery
And how emancipation did not set us free.

The old oak told of the mighty Mississippi
The one Great-Grandpa swore was the River Nile
Come, Old Man River, spread your wings
Send forth your sons
To the north, east, west, and south.

The old oak told of Grandma Nettie's wedding
Under the harvest moon
It told of the country mornings
Fresh and sweet with dew.

The old oak told of the crimson roses
Of the acorn and what it will be
My son like the acorn must pass under the branches
And listen to the old oak tree.

/

I sit out in the lonely sea
Formed not found
No future
No destiny
A sea of loneliness
That surrounds me
A sea of tranquility
That astounds me
A sea of sounds
That whisper
My every plea
A sea of vision
That sees the inner me
A sea of thoughts
Beckoning near and far
To come closer
To discover me
The Isle of Man

IN A SHALLOW STREAM

In a shallow stream
I once went sailing
To the sea and beyond
It carried me.

From that shallow stream
To a world of dreams
It carried me
Much further
Than the stars.

IN MY HOUR OF MADNESS

In my hour of madness
I cannot see my face
Memory of yesterday's sadness
Leaving loneliness
And empty space.

A faceless name
And hurting pain
Are the things
That I have kept.
The cold winter rains
Have come again
As my pillow wept.

IN TIME

In time
The seasons slowly pass
Spring has yielded to summer
The fall harvest is stored away
I see the wild geese in their V-wedge
In time
They slowly pass away.

INSEPARABLE

Inseparable
That's what we are
Like the shadow
That follows the sun
The stream that flows to the sea
And beyond
Inseparable
That's what we are
Friends sworn as one
A kaleidoscope with the sun
Like the sand and sea
We melt as one
Inseparable
That's what we are.

IT IS SAID

It is said
The rumblings
Of spring
Are the awakenings
Of the gods
After their slumber
Of winter.

IT RAINED TODAY

It rained today
A soft and gentle thing
And on my roof
It came alive.

Very gently it tapped
A love song
A swan song
A song of the heart.

And then the wind came
Joining the rain
And as one they danced
On my roof through the night.

And when the morning came
I went to the door
The rain bent and kissed my face
And the wind gently
Took it away.

IT RAINED TONIGHT

It rained tonight,
I felt the wetness
On my pillow.

ETERNAL LOVE

It was a cold December day
The day her spirit flew away
We love her but she couldn't stay
Gretchen went home for Christmas.

The angels rejoiced when she arrived
St. Peter greeted her at the appointed time
No more Christmas shopping or waiting in line
Gretchen, welcome home for Christmas.

St. Peter, what about the ones I left behind?
Their hearts are broken and need mending time
Family, if you could only see me now
I made it home for Christmas.

To my family and friends, I love you true
Jesus brought me home, and he'll bring you too
I've completed my journey, and now you must walk yours through
I'll see you soon for Christmas.
Eternal Love, Gretchen

I'VE SEEN TREE LEAVES

I've seen tree leaves blow in the wind
But never have they blown like this before
So gentle, nearly still,
But never so gentle as this before.
I've spent hours watching the clouds roll by
But never have they rolled like this before
Beautiful white ships on canvas of blue
But never so white or blue before.
I've walked in a tropical rain and been renewed
But never have I been renewed like this before
I've seen a rainbow pierce the southern moon
But never have I seen a rainbow like this before.
I've lain in a hammock and observed the stars afar
But never have I seen stars like this before
Stars so bright with heavenly glow
But never so bright as this before.
I've kissed my wife a thousand times
But never have I kissed her like this before
A kiss that refused to be held by time
But never has she kissed me like this before.

JUST TO HEAR THE ANGELS SING

Just to hear the angels sing
Joined in by church bell rings

Just to see an angel fly
To soar like an eagle in the sky

Just to touch an angel's heart
Is to receive God's undeserved reward

Tears of joy from an angel's eye
Is to feel the soft rain from the Texas sky.

LET'S GO BACK TO WEEDY PARK

Let's go back to Weedy Park
Back to baseball and hide-and-go-seek
Pathways through our urban jungle
Have led to my destiny
In Weedy Park
I learned how to win
And when I lost
To pick myself up
Dust it off
And start over again
I owned my first house
In Weedy Park
It was made of cardboard
Mud and such
And our cabin in the sky
A tree house with a view
And when it was time to depart
A rope elevator delivered me to the floor
Of Weedy Park.

LIGHTNING BUGS AND SUMMER NIGHTS

Lightning bugs and summer nights
Honeysuckle and mosquito bites
Bullfrogs and crickets on the pond
Weenie roasts and chewing gum
Baseball and riding bikes
Boy Scout camp and summer hikes
Swimming pools and diving boards
Summertime fun never bored
Bible school and sack lunches
My favorite blackberry patch juicy bunches
Sleeping out under the stars
Fell while skating add to the scars
Paper route get started before dawn
Sleepy in church better cover that yawn
Pulled the pigtails of the girl I didn't like
She hit me back and smiled her dislike
It's a full life being ten
Summertime fun hanging out with my friends.

LIKE THE ROSE THAT WENT UNPICKED

Like the rose that went unpicked
He died on the vine

The morning dew kissed his crimson petals
As he bled for all mankind

The water gushed from the wounds in his side
This water he would not turn to wine

The wilted rose that went unpicked
Like Jesus, bloomed in three days' time.

LITTLE BOY

Little boy
What are you doing down there
Just remember
I'll always care
When you fall
And cut your knee
I can't always be there
To dry your eyes.

Little boy
When you start to school
My son, do not forget
The golden rule
You are your brother's keeper
And to do less
Would make you weaker
Than the man I hope
You will become.

LOVE IS

Love is
More precious than
Each raindrop
Fallen upon
The shore.

EVERLASTING

Now that I've found you
It is to hold a dream
For a million years

To kiss a thought
Before it passes

To love a memory
That will never fade

To wish upon a star
Trying to bring it back

To cry in misery
Trying not to look ahead

ONE LAST STROLL DOWN MEMORY LANE

One last stroll down memory lane
We'll talk and visit in the shade
We'll talk what was and what might have been
Of school, summertime, and old girlfriends.

Remember when we started to school
We made a promise to follow the golden rules
Who knew our pact would last fifty years to the day
And we would walk again down Old Magnolia Way.

We cut our fingers and joined our blood
We became blood brothers against the world
You hurt one and the other felt the pain
That was our pact made on Old Magnolia Lane.

Remember when we learned to swim
Or shot our first basket in a gym
My first date, not knowing what to say
It all began down Old Magnolia Way.

The lane is dusty now and the way is dim
Memories abound, where went the years?
Our children laugh and we smile it away
For they too one day must walk down Old Magnolia Way.

REMEMBER ME

Remember me
As you continue through time
And when you think
Of the good old days
While on your journey in the past
Think of the love
We once shared
Of the days just walking
Hand in hand.

On cold nights
And warm remembrances
I will think of you
For those were
Good times,
Happy times,
Sad times,
Our time.

FROM THE MOUNTAIN

Rushing from the mountain
Down to the sea
Our love passes forth
Onward to the outer sea,
At times it rages
As a sea of storm,
But then it can be quiet
The smoothest of sail,
A comforting love
Of future days past
Everlasting love
Not cornered
But as free as the sea
And forever
Engulfed by time.

SEPTEMBER DREAM

September dream
Is a time for winter thoughts,
Of summer days gone
Feeling lazy days of Indian summer
While lying in golden fields
With the wind on one's face,
Seeing reflections disappear
At the toss of a stone,
Or strolling with a hidden love
Held in one's heart,
Seeing red, yellow, and gold
Hues of my rainbow
As they reflect,
September dream.

SKY IS HIS GREATNESS

Sky is his greatness
So is the sea
Eyes of eagles
For him to see
Minds of men
For him to think
Shallow streams
For him to drink
Wings of birds
For him to fly
To soar far
Beyond the sky
He watches the world
From mountain peaks
The valleys are his
To rest and sleep
He eats and drinks
From Mother Nature's breast
His greatness is supreme
There is no test.

SLOWLY I RUSHED

Slowly I rushed the sea
For it would come only so close to me
I felt its gentle breath upon my cheek
Softly, so very softly it whispered,
Come, come where the sun never sets
And the mornings are milky with dew
Come, come lie in my secret oasis,
And so very gently I came.

SOMEWHERE THERE IS A LOVE FOR ME

Somewhere there is a love for me
She awaits my loving call
She sits and listens
The birds sing
Our love song
From nature's choir.
When sleep is near
We pause to rest
Among the lilies
And daffodils
We lay our heads
On golden hay
While the lark plays
Its melody.
Good night, children of the sun
Rest thyself for the day is done
The sun will soon be up
And once again
Thy shadow
You will give chase
So sleep, children of the sun.

THAT OLD TREE

That old tree
Bent with age
Some branches have
Yielded to nature
The others have
Stood the test of time
That old tree
I defied gravity
Under its canopy
I swung out into space
And back to earth
Again and again.

That old tree
Heard my woes
And listened when
No one understood
My pain
And when I cried
It dried my eyes
Its leaves with the wind
Would sing me a lullaby
That old tree
Is where I first glimpsed integrity
It stands with its head unbowed
Golden leaves of autumn as a crown.

LIFE'S MYSTERIES

The answer to life's mysteries
Lies in oneself
Do not look for it
In others
Or you will fool yourself
Search hard and long
Until you find your way
The answer lies in oneself
Do not delay
If not around the corner
Seek and you shall find
The answer to life's mysteries
Is not so easily found
There are many
And yes they are profound
But the answer
Lies in oneself
Seek and you shall find

THE BEAUTY OF THE ROSE

The beauty of the rose
But so deadly to the touch
The grace of an eagle in flight
As the hare runs in fright.

So pure the thought
Yet so deadly the action
With the ease of thought
Most life will stalk
The wonder and beauty
Of nature.

THE COLOR OF FLOWERS IN MAY

The color of flowers in May
The smell of new-mowed hay

The smile of a daffodil
The sun as it comes over a hill

The sea when it kisses the shore
Puppies wagging their tails begging for more

The fragrance of June roses in full bloom
The beauty of night under a Texas moon

A sudden downpour in the middle of July
Precious angel tears falling from the Texas sky

The morning rolls over and heaves a sigh
As the Texas star lost to day winks bye bye.

THE CRICKET SONG

The cricket sang
Its summer song
Each night
It serenaded
The moon.

The bullfrog
Joined in
And oh what a blend
They made music
On the pond.

THE DOVE AND SPARROW

The dove and sparrow
Sleep in the tree at night
One sings, the other chirps
At the coming of first light.

It's going to be a beautiful morning
Mr. Sparrow
Mr. Dove, I do believe you're right
Let's go have breakfast at Worm's
Let's go have a bite.

THE EARLY MORNING FOG

The early morning fog
Disappears with the tides
Gone away, gone away.

The shadows trying to
Outrace the sun
Gone away, gone away.

The sea when it parts from
The shore
Gone away, gone away.

The clouds when they cry
Tears of joy
Gone away, gone away.

The gentle rains that kissed my lips
My face skyward yearning for another sip
Suddenly!
Gone away, gone away.

THE GENTLE TUG

The gentle tug upon my sleeve
Was much more than the summer breeze
Your sacred dance brought to life
The crowning of our King.

The dance of life you slowly wove
Your offering unto the Lord
Flung to the floor you lay prostrate
Your offering unto the Lord.

Your dance was not for silver or gold
It was a tapestry woven with love,
You bowed as the heavens opened
Your offering unto the Lord.

GOLDEN LEAVES

The golden leaves
Of autumn's trees
Are quickly
Turned to brown
Managed by the wind
And tossed to the ground
The birds fly south
The chill from the north
Lifeless days
And lonely nights
Spent in contemplation
Of you.

THE REMEDY TREE

Branches and switches
Are one and the same
I was a horticulturist
Before I could spell my name
My mother would have me prune the Remedy tree
Several times a week
She told me the pruning would make me stronger
The pruning would not make me weak.

The tree grew bigger and stronger
And so did I
Like the tree, I learned how to yield to the wind
And bend to the changing tides
So, my son, when I ask you to prune the Remedy tree
Don't hesitate, bring me the switch
The pruning will make you stronger
The pruning will not make you weak.

THE SILENCE YOU'VE GIVEN TO ME

The silence you've
Given to me,
Fallen leaves
From autumn's tree,
For when I walk
On nature's floor,
You speak of things
That came before
You tell me of
Long-lost loves,
And of the victories
That were won
You tell the coming
Of winter's rains,
And of the ones
Who died in vain
These are the things
You've given to me,
And why leaves fall
From autumn's tree.

SOFT AND GENTLE RAIN

The soft and gentle rain
Is my friend
And follows
Wherever I go
It whispers in my ear
And lightly caresses my hair
It follows me wherever I go
It follows me on the pavement
And around each corner it greets me
We run and play in the park
I slip in the grass
And as it picks me up
We laugh
And when it is time to go
It follows me to my door
The soft and gentle rain
Is my friend.

FEELS GOOD

The sun feels good
The bee with all its venom
Touches the scented flower,
Rupturing its virginity.

The flower, welcoming the touch
Of a unknown lover,
Came into full bloom
Spreading its petals
And fragrance.

THE WILLOW

The willow
Will weep no more
Only in love songs
Does it have
Teary eyes.

THE WIND BLOWS STRONGLY IN NOVEMBER

The wind blows strongly in November
No longer is the bloom on the vine
The cold has captured the winter flower
In its bitter embrace held frozen in time.

The wind blows strongly in November
The trees are barren and stark
In their nakedness they sway
With the wind they say
It's a beautiful winter day.

THE YOU THAT I SEE

The you that I see
Woman-child of mystery
A caged bird
That must be set free
This is the you I see.

The you that I see
Tall, bronzed, eternally,
With a child's heart
And a woman's mind,
Not a contradiction,
The you that I see.

THERE IS A SEASON

There is a season
Where flowers bloom forever
Why lovers never have to say I'm sorry
You and I walk hand in hand.

Under the darkened sky
Our love lights up the night
Love protects us from the freight
Of having to be apart.

We'll stay together
And stay in love forever
Never having to say we're sorry
For being in love this way.

You and I are the reason
Where love lasts forever
Where flowers bloom forever
You and I walk hand in hand.

THERE YOU SIT

There you sit
With the greenest of eye
Set in platinum
Gold and despair
Men have sold
Their souls and more
To possess you,
The greenest of eye.

All was peaceful
When you slept undisturbed
A blanket of earth
To keep you warm,
Once unearthed
Your eye has captured
And now devours.

TIME IS A ROBBER

Time is a robber
Yesterday a lingering thief
Things set aside
Now lie wasted at your feet.

The dreams of your youth
Carried down through the years
Still held in one's heart
All of fifty years.

Time is a robber
Today without relief
I did not have time for my children
Now, they do not have time for me.

So do not put off another day
Tomorrow may not come your way
For time is a robber
Tomorrow a better thief.

TO REMEMBER

To remember the fights
Of glory past
A love lost
Among the fallen stars
Somewhere a flower blossoms
Among the living dead
We seek the instance
Of our beginning.
From the mountains
Where eagles dare
Off the breeze
It is whispered
The coming rains
Will cry the tears
And the coming
Of distant drums.
As the laughter
In the night
Brings to each
The morning sun
We must surrender
Unto life
Where the sea
Rests against the shore.

TO THE MARINER

To the mariner,
If you do not
Find love
The sea will
Not reject you,
For it longs to
Hold you
In its
Cold embrace.

TO THE SEA

To the sea
You have gone
The lonely mariner
So all alone
To cast your nets
Beyond the reef
Trying to capture love.

LOST IN A SEA OF STORMS

Two people lost in a sea of storms,
Beneath the waves
From whence they come,
Only to surface
To consummate their love,
They return to the depths,
Everlasting.

WE SET FORTH

We set forth
In times of trouble
Knowing not which way to go
Seeing the hate
That surrounds us
Helps to make us stronger.

We search for truth
Among the lies
As we tread the narrow way
With truth and wisdom
Visioned in the sky
We follow God's righteous path.

We walk from darkness
Into the light
Feeling the love
That surrounds us
This light of love
He put in our hearts
Helps to make us stronger.

WE

We're going to see Grandma
Way down in the country
Off the blacktop road
Where the melons
Are big and juicy
Just the other side
Of the cotton patch.
I can hear the women folks
Humming and cooking
I sit out back and listen
To the men just a talking
Cousin Coochie got that
Old pump primed and a crying
Way down in the country
Off the blacktop road.
We throw dirt clods
At the cows and each other
Got a bee sting
Grandma used snuff
To remove the poison
Here comes our fighting cousin
Looking for trouble
Down in the country
Off the blacktop road.
Got to go, wish I could stay
Just a little bit longer
With my family here
I'm never lonely
Grab a hug
Show some love
Shout good-bye
See you next time.

Bye, Grandma, Cousin Vernon,
Aunt Robby, Uncle Jay, Coochie
And to all the others,
Until we meet again
Down in the country
Off the blacktop road.

INTO THIS WORLD

When I came into this world
I was greeted by your smile
You cared for and nurtured me
Sometimes with a smile
Or a switch to my behind
When I disappointed
With love you admonished
But you never denied
Your love or time
Trudging through the snow
You provided for me
Always with love
For your baby boy
You guided me.

Although you've departed
Your earthly home
The breath of life
You gave to me
I must carry on.

INTO THE STILL OF THE NIGHT

When I look into the still of the night
The trees are glassy and white
A spectrum of colors, brown, yellow, red and evergreen
All are covered with ice.

A frozen rainbow, announcing winter's arrival
Silent sentinels with smiles frozen in place
I look with awe, knowing after the thaw,
You'll still be rooted in the same place.

The streetlights reflect off you
As if you were some high-priced chandelier
Your limbs sway and seem to know
Of the music that is about to unfold.

A light tinkling sound, nature's wind chimes
Resound each time your limbs try to embrace
With squirrels and birds tucked near
I wonder if they hear
The music of your tiny frozen waterfalls.

WHEN I LOOKED INTO HER EYES

When I looked into her eyes
There was so much love and a little surprise
She would say the apple doesn't fall far from the tree
Me, I would look guilty, for she knew I was both good and bad,
Then she would hug me.

Grandma Nettie picked more cotton than any two grown men
And come spring, chop three rows of cotton out of every ten
Every now and then she would lean on her hoe
Take a dip, wink a smile, then start chopping some more.

Come evening time as the women prepared supper
You could hear her talking to my mother, aunts, and sisters
Knowledge passed from my great grandmother she imparted.

When the stars came out, she would walk over to the well
I think she liked to hear the sound of that old pump
Crying as it released its water into the night
The taste of that well water with its rusty flavor
The coldest, best-tasting water this side of heaven.

I suppose by today's standard
She would be called a superwoman,
We just called her Grandma Nettie
And we all loved her.

WHEN I SEE BUTTERFLIES

When I see butterflies fluttering in a meadow
I think of angels playing in the clouds of heaven

When I feel the gentle wind upon my cheek
My angel is telling me to remain humble and meek

When I see a rainbow smile upside down
It's my angel standing on his head being a clown

When I hear water over a fall, birds chirping and bees humming,
It's my angel leading nature's choir with the beaver's tail a thumping.

WHEN SEASONS CHANGE

When seasons change forever
And love goes away
The breeze will stir
Each fallen leaf
The birds
Will fly away
The streams will
Flow freely
Upon stones untouched
By time
The water will
Wash cleanly
All the sands
Of time.

SWEET NORA BROWN

She came from the sea into my life
This is the tale of Sweet Nora Brown,
Black as the night over an angry sea
She rode a wave of love onto the shore.

The birds will tell of Sweet Nora Brown
Go out and listen amongst the trees,
The bees hum at the mention of her name
Her name taste like honey to me

Sweet Nora Brown wears a crown
Of tulips, dandelions, and one daffodil,
She sits on her throne a grassy knoll
Longingly looking out to sea.

Rabbits come to play at her feet
For her a bear danced and grin
Sweet Nora blew a kiss and a butterfly it became
It fluttered and brought the kiss to me.

Sweet Nora Brown wears a crown
But no longer look out to sea
The birds tell wherever they fly
How Sweet Nora now only look for me..

WHEN THE MORNING

When the morning sun
Streaks your hair with gold
When the new
Becomes the old
And when we stand before God
Our lives will unfold
No truer act of love
Will be told
When the wind
Is blowing free
Across the sand
And beyond the sea
And when the wine
Has turn to kisses
Out of night
Will have taken day.

WHEN WINTER COMES

When winter comes
Still life replaces
The hustle
Of summer day.

WHERE DO TEARDROPS GO

Where do teardrops go
When they fall upon the floor?
Do they escape to the sea?
Or become nectar for the bee?
Tell me, where do teardrops go?

Where do teardrops go?
Do they wander up and down the shore?
Like the ancient mariner, do they look out to sea?
Once released, are they still a part of me?
Tell me, where do teardrops go?

Where do teardrops go?
Do they help make the flowers grow?
Are they the ending, or a new beginning?
Can they help mend a broken heart?
Tell me, where do teardrops go?

MEMORY LANE

While walking down memory lane
I passed through cotton fields and sugar cane
Tossed a rock in my favorite fishing hole
Picked blackberries from a patch of old
As I walked with my childhood friends
One shouted tag, and you're it again.
A light breeze carried smells from out the kitchen door
Curly barked and joined us with a mighty roar
Every now and then it's nice to go home again
For you see these memories are some of my dearest friends.

WITHOUT LOVE'S ANSWER

Without love's answer
Close at hand
I began to chase
As it ran.
Far from me
It quickly passed,
To eternal limbo
Only to return
Again and again.

YOU ARE THE BERRY

You are the berry
That stained my hand,
I picked and now
Shall devour.

REMNANT

You are the remnant at my feet
Rise angel ballerina and dance for me
Spread your wings for the whole world to see
Where I brought you from.

Some thought you had faded away
Like the black of night to the pale gray of day
But I said I would restore you this day
A remnant of what will be.

A broken mirror on the floor
Into many thousands of pieces
Swept out the door
Only I see what the mirror could not behold
A jigsaw puzzle restored.

Tattered, torn, and bloodied from your past
These remnants are the garments of salvation you must wear
I am your God I sent for thee
Angel ballerina, come dance for me.

YOU ARE

You are the wildflower
That I would love
To plunder,
Open your petals
And let me in.

YOU CAN NEVER GO HOME AGAIN

You can never go home again.
Many have tried but they never quite get there.
There is a mall where the old school once stood,
The bike path, now a four-lane highway.
Well, at least they followed the kids on that one,
But it will never take you back to your door.

I once knew of a great man, now he is small.
I would like to remember him as he was,
But the pathway back will not let him be that
Which he was.

Where we once played king of the mountain
Is now just a hill,
And the old stream, so wide, so deep
Now you can hop and get to the other side.

No, I want go back.
Let the mountain remain a mountain
The stream as wide as the sea
And the great man, let him stand as he once stood.

I can still see the place where the old oak
looked out upon the world.
My first kiss was there, and there I took refuge
When the kiss was broken.
No, I will never go back.

AUTHOR BIOGRAPHY

D. Carver Brazwell is the proud father of three adult children, and re-sides in the Dallas/Ft. Worth metroplex with his wife of twenty-seven years, Glinda. A graduate of The University of Texas at Dallas, he holds a Bachelor's of Art in Political Science. His favorite hobby is riding his motorcycle. You may contact him at deaconcorner@sbcglobal.net.

Printed in the United States
By Bookmasters